ASHLEY STORM

BAD DAY

LIFESKILLS IN ACTION

SOFT SKILLS

SADDLEBACK
EDUCATIONAL PUBLISHING
www.sdlback.com

ISBN: 978-1-68021-942-5
eBook: 978-1-64598-357-6

Printed in Malaysia

25 24 23 22 21   1 2 3 4 5

Tara should have stayed in bed. Nothing went right all day.

The trouble started before school. Tara could not find her sneakers. Then she saw one. Her stomach sank. It was in the dog's water bowl. Peanut had destroyed it.

Tara picked up the wet sneaker. It dripped with water and slobber. She dropped it in the garbage can. The second shoe was nowhere to be seen.

Ugh, Tara thought. *This day can't get any worse.*

She was wrong.

There was a quiz in first period. Tara failed it.

In third period, she dropped her pencil. It rolled across the room. Tara stood to get it. The teacher told her to sit down.

That was so unfair. How could she work without a pencil?

Then came lunch. It was spaghetti day.
Things were finally looking up. Tara loved
pasta. The sauce looked delicious. Cheese
was sprinkled on top. She could not wait
to dive in.

Tara reached for her fork. Someone yelled.
She looked up.

Two boys were wrestling. They crashed into her table. Tara's plate slid into her lap. Spaghetti flew everywhere. There was none left to eat. Everyone laughed. But Tara didn't. It was not funny to her.

The day was a disaster. Tara wanted to go home. But there was still band practice.

Marching band was fun. They performed at football games.

Tara played trumpet. She had a great solo. Nothing was better than playing for a crowd.

Still, her heart was not in it today. She was hungry. Her pants were a mess. Dried spaghetti sauce covered them.

Tara got her trumpet from her locker. She trudged into the band room. Skyler was already there, tuning her trumpet.

That was weird. Her best friend was never early. Skyler did not see her come in.

"I have had the worst day." Tara plopped down next to Skyler. She opened her trumpet case.

"Oh?" Skyler chewed on a thumbnail. Tara had never seen her do that.

"When did you start biting your nails?" Tara did not wait for an answer. She talked about her day. It felt good to complain.

Skyler frowned. "I'm sorry you had a bad day."

Tara sighed. "At least it's over."

Skyler nibbled on her pinky nail. "I need to tell you something."

Mr. Key whistled. Tara and Skyler turned to face their teacher.

"Before we start today's practice, we have a challenge."

Everyone gasped. That meant someone was trying for a better part. There could not be a winner without a loser.

Tara raised her eyebrows at Skyler. Her friend looked at the floor.

Mr. Key cleared his throat. "Skyler is challenging Tara for the trumpet solo."

Tara's mouth fell open. She stared at her friend. Skyler did not look at her. The day kept getting worse.

"You know how this works," Mr. Key said. "Skyler will play first. Then Tara will play. The band will choose the winner."

Skyler pressed the trumpet to her lips. Her tone was perfect. She hit every note. Tara had never heard Skyler play so well.

Soon, it was her turn. Tara's heart raced. Her arms shook. It was hard to breathe.

Her fingers were clumsy. They moved too fast. She flubbed some notes.

The band voted for Skyler. Tara tried not to cry.

After that, the band moved to the practice field. Skyler tried to talk to Tara. But Tara just ignored her.

Practice was awful. Tara was out of step. The trumpet seemed heavier than usual. Her tongue did not work. She sounded terrible.

Finally, practice ended.

Tara walked home alone. Tears welled up in her eyes.

Of all things, Tara thought her solo was safe. But Skyler had stolen it. Should Tara have seen this coming? Were there signs?

Skyler was chewing her nails before practice. Why? Had she been nervous? *Nervous about stealing my part*, Tara thought.

At home, Peanut ran to greet Tara. Her missing shoe dangled from his mouth. His tail wagged happily. She could not stay mad at her dog. He did not mean to ruin her day. Dogs did not know better. But people did.

How could Skyler do this? Tara fell onto her bed. She screamed into her pillow. They were supposed to be best friends. Skyler did not even warn her.

Tara squeezed her eyes shut. It did not stop the tears. She had told Skyler about her bad day. But Skyler just made it worse. *Who does that? An ex-best friend, that's who.*

She pulled her phone from her pocket. There were many photos of Skyler. Tara scrolled through and deleted them one by one. It felt good.

Her favorite picture filled the screen. It was taken at a football game. She and Skyler were both grinning. They wore their band uniforms. Their arms were wrapped around each other.

The girls looked so happy in the picture. Music was Tara's favorite thing. But Skyler loved it just as much. That was one of the reasons they were friends.

She could not delete the photo. It was too special.

Tara tried to see the situation through her friend's eyes. Both of them loved the solo. They practiced it together all the time. Skyler's challenge was unexpected. But why? Challenges were part of band.

A tear rolled down Tara's cheek. She wiped it away and sat up.

Skyler had not stolen her part. She won fair and square. Tara had lost control of her emotions. It cost her the solo. That was her fault, not Skyler's.

Tara pulled up Skyler's phone number and sent her the picture. Then she sent a text. "Are you home? Can I come over?"

"Sure," Skyler texted back.

It took ten minutes to walk to Skyler's house. Tara considered her feelings. Her anger was gone. But she was still sad. The solo had meant a lot to her. Losing it was hard.

She also felt embarrassed. The whole band voted against her. They knew she could play well. But Skyler was better today.

Shame filled her. It had been dumb to delete pictures of Skyler. Some pictures were from school. Others were from sleepovers. One was a selfie with Peanut. There were so many. But the photos were gone. Now they were just memories.

Tara arrived at Skyler's house. After taking a deep breath, she knocked.

Skyler opened the door. "Hey."

"Can I come in?" Tara asked. She kicked the ground with the toe of her shoe.

Skyler nodded. She led Tara to her room. Sheet music covered her bed. Her trumpet rested on a pillow.

"Your solo was great today," Tara said. "You deserved to win."

Skyler's cheeks turned red. "Sorry I didn't say anything. You should have heard about it from me first."

Tara shrugged. "It's okay."

"No," Skyler said. "I was going to tell you, but . . ." Her voice trailed off.

"I would not shut up about my day," Tara finished.

Skyler tucked her hair behind her ears. "I'm sorry for making your day worse."

Tara shook her head. "It's not your fault. My emotions got the best of me. That won't happen again." Her eyes locked onto Skyler's. "You will be amazing at Friday's game. I know it."

"But let me guess. You are coming for me on Monday?"

"Sorry," Tara said, smiling. "I want my solo back."

Skyler grinned. "Bring it."

Just then, Tara's stomach growled loudly. They both burst out laughing. Everything would be okay. Tara wanted the solo. But she *needed* her best friend.

"Want to stay for dinner?" Skyler asked. "We're having your favorite."

Tara's eyes opened wide. She looked down at her stained jeans. "You mean spaghetti?"

Skyler chuckled. "And meatballs. Maybe you will get some in your mouth this time."

Tara raised her eyebrows. "Is that a challenge?"

Skyler nodded. "Yep."

"I see," Tara said. Then she laughed. "Challenge accepted."

Knowing yourself and how you react in certain situations puts you in control. It also helps you better understand others. That's what emotional intelligence is all about. Want to learn how you can understand your emotions and better sense how others are feeling?

JUST *flip* THE BOOK!

LIFESKILLS IN ACTION

Emotional Intelligence

JILL L.
HANEY

LIFESKILLS IN ACTION

SOFT SKILLS

SADDLEBACK
EDUCATIONAL PUBLISHING
www.sdlback.com

ISBN: 978-1-68021-942-5
eBook: 978-1-64598-357-6

Printed in Malaysia

25 24 23 22 21   1 2 3 4 5

It has been a **bad day.**

First Liz woke up late.

She missed the bus and ran to school.

That took half an hour.

Liz rushed to class.

But she was still tardy.

Now school is out.

Liz sits in detention.

The clock ticks.

She taps her foot.

Her friends are having fun without her.

This is so boring, Liz thinks.

It's not fair.

The teacher looks at her.

"Do your work, Liz."

"Or what?" she snaps.

"I want out of here."

The teacher is angry.

"That was rude.

You just got more detention.

Come back here tomorrow."

"No!" Liz yells.

What went wrong in this story?

Liz **lost control.**

She didn't manage her time well.

Then her feelings boiled over.

Managing emotions is not easy.

First you must identify them.

This is part of **emotional intelligence.**

It starts with knowing yourself.

How do you feel?

Figure that out.

Then choose how to act.

Be smart about it.

That puts you in control.

There's more to emotional intelligence.

It's also about sensing how others feel.

This helps you talk to them.

You can choose the right words.

All this takes work.

Look at yourself first.

Who are you inside?

What do you want most?

Knowing this is **self-awareness.**

We all have feelings.

It's part of being human.

They may come in a rush.

That can overwhelm us.

SAD
EMBARRASSED
STRESSED
TIRED
AFRAID
HOPELESS

EXHAUSTED
WORRIED
MAD
DEPRESSED
NERVOUS
CONCERNED

You can be ready for this.

Find a quiet place.

Think back.

Picture a time when emotions took over.

What caused it?

How did you react?

Reflecting helps.

It makes you mindful.

This leads to better choices.

Learn what upsets you.

Prepare for it.

Avoid it if possible.

Knowing ourselves is powerful.

It puts us in control.

We decide how to react.

This is called **self-management.**

Stress is part of life.

It can be good.

We do something new.

Our bodies react.

At first, we may get nervous.

But then we learn.

Tasks get easier.

Too much stress is not good.

It can make us freeze.

We may not be able to focus.

Life feels overwhelming.

That may make us lash out.

Self-management helps.

It **reduces stress.**

We know what upsets us.

Then we can work to fix it.

Picture this.

Tom is on the bus.

It gets loud.

Noise irritates him.

He knows this about himself.

That helps him plan.

Tom puts in earbuds.

He listens to songs he likes.

They block out the noise.

This helps Tom stay calm.

Managing his stress works.

Stress can lead to poor choices.

A man has a long day at work.

He stops to shop.

Candy is up front.

It is easy to grab some.

A student has homework.

She needs to write a paper.

Her phone buzzes.

Checking texts is more fun.

Want to hang out today?

These are **impulses.**

Everyone has them.

Something looks good.

You want it.

But you don't need it.

Take a step back.

Reflect.

Why do you want the item?

Are you feeling low?

It may seem like a good idea now.

But you could regret it later.

Deal with the emotion.

Sleep on it.

See how you feel later.

This is how to **take control.**

Being self-aware makes life easier.

We get why we do things.

It helps us understand others too.

Clues become clear.

A person may stare into space.

Their lips are turned down.

We sense they are sad.

Our gut says to comfort them.

This is **social awareness.**

It's figuring out how others feel.

That takes practice.

But knowing ourselves helps.

We are more sensitive to others.

Listening helps too.

This is not just hearing.

It is taking an active part.

Give others your **attention.**

Focus on their faces.

Set aside devices.

Note how they say things.

Watch for other **clues.**

A man may tap his foot.

He talks quickly.

You see him look at his watch.

Maybe he is impatient.

A woman gives a big smile.

She speaks loudly.

Her hands move as she talks.

It's likely she is excited.

Being socially aware pays off.

We pick up on feelings.

Then we know how to react.

People appreciate this.

They like to be understood.

This is **empathy.**

It means to feel what others feel.

Empathy helps us make friends.

We see someone else's side.

That can draw them to us.

Here is an example.

Kat is a new student.

She goes to math class.

Mel sits by her.

She searches her backpack.

"Where is it?" Mel mutters.

Kat hears this.

She smiles kindly.

"Hi. I'm Kat.

Do you need a pencil?"

"Yes," Mel says.

"How did you know?"

"It was a good guess," Kat says.

"I have an extra.

Here you go.

You can keep it."

"Thanks! I'm Mel.

Lunch is after this class.

My friends have a table.

Come sit with us."

Kat grins. "Cool."

Being a new student is not easy.

But Kat is socially aware.

She shows empathy.

That helps her **make a friend.**

Relationships take work.

Emotions play a big role.

Understanding them is key.

It builds trust.

How can you get along with others?

Lift them up.

Show your support.

Happiness spreads.

It will come back to you.

Accept others.

Let them be themselves.

Open up.

Show the real you.

Sometimes people argue.

There is **conflict.**

Understanding emotions helps.

Look at all sides.

Figure out how they are feeling.

Ask why.

Let each person talk.

Then come up with a plan.

Stay positive.

Make sure everyone agrees.

Think about your life.

What makes you happy?

It starts with emotional intelligence.

Knowing who you are is key.

Be aware of your feelings.

Work through them.

Take control.

Then **reach out** to others.

Look for clues as to how they feel.

Help when you can.

People will appreciate it.

You may even make new friends.

I was quick to react.

JUST *Flip* THE BOOK!

ASHLEY STORM

BAD DAY

Tara doesn't think her day can get any worse. But Tara soon realizes she's wrong when her best friend competes with her for something they both want. Find out how Tara reacts in *Bad Day*. Want to read on?